THE LIBRARY OF WEAPONS OF MASS DESTRUCTION™

The Search for Weapons of Mass Destruction in Iraq

BARBARA MOE

The Rosen Publishing Group, Inc., New York

Dedicated to all those who work for world peace and the elimination of weapons of mass destruction

Published in 2005 by The Rosen Publishing Group, Inc.
29 East 21st Street, New York, NY 10010

First Edition

Library of Congress Cataloging-in-Publication Data

Moe, Barbara A.
The search for weapons of mass destruction in Iraq / Barbara Moe.
   p. cm. — (The library of weapons of mass destruction)
Includes bibliographical references and index.
ISBN 1-4042-0295-1 (library binding)
1. Weapons of mass destruction—Iraq—Juvenile. literature. 2. Iraq War,
2003—Juvenile literature.
I. Title. II. Series.
U793.M64 2004
956.7044'31—dc22
                                                    2004014485

Manufactured in the United States of America

On the cover: U.S. soldiers in chemical protective suits search an industrial complex in the Iraqi town of Baquba on May 1, 2003, for weapons of mass destruction.

[CONTENTS]

INTRODUCTION

Twice since 1991, the United States has gone to war against the Middle Eastern nation of Iraq. The first time, the United States was responding to a flagrant act of aggression by Iraq against one of its neighbors, the tiny, oil-rich nation of Kuwait. Citing old and new grievances against Kuwait, Iraq's dictatorial president, Saddam Hussein, had sent Iraq's armed forces to invade Kuwait.

With its own small military no match for Iraq's, Kuwait asked for help from the United States and

A man stands among the rusted remains of missile heads in February 2003. Officials in Baghdad showed the remains to UN inspectors and told them that the missile heads at one time contained biological weapons before being destroyed in 1991 to meet the requirements of UN resolutions at the time.

the United Nations (UN). With virtually the entire world outraged by Iraq's action, the United States was quickly able to assemble a coalition of nations willing to provide military force against Iraq. The United States itself sent more than 500,000 troops to the region; they were joined by forces from many other countries, most notably Great Britain and France. U.S. bombing of Iraq began on January 17, 1991. By the end of February, Iraq's troops had been driven from Kuwait. With the exception of a handful of states, the entire world agreed that the Gulf War had been a just one and that the U.S. response to Iraq's actions had been fitting and justified. Within the United States, the greatest debate about the war centered on whether U.S. troops should continue into Iraq once the Iraqis had been dislodged from Kuwait, and carry the war on to Baghdad, Iraq's capital, with the purpose of ousting Hussein from power. President George H. W. Bush ultimately decided not to take direct military action to oust Hussein at that time.

World opinion was much less united about the second Gulf War. In opposition to the wishes of the UN and with minimal support from other nations, the United States invaded Iraq on March 19, 2003, with the purpose of driving Hussein from power. U.S. forces overwhelmed the Iraqi military in less than three weeks. On December 13, 2003, Hussein was captured by the U.S. Army. U.S. troops and government agencies settled in for a tumultuous period of occupation and reconstruction of Iraq.

This time, however, response to the U.S. action was much more hostile. Several of the staunchest allies of the United States, most notably Germany and France, refused to take part in the invasion. Opposition to the U.S. invasion in other European countries was fierce. Arab nations that had supported the first Gulf War condemned the U.S. actions this time. Opinion polls showed virtually worldwide opposition to the U.S. invasion.

What had changed? The greatest difference was the reasons the United States had given for going to war. In the first Gulf War, the United States was responding to an outrageous act that had taken place: Iraq's invasion of Kuwait. In the second Gulf War, many people found the justification the United States gave for its action much less clear and convincing. In this case, the United States said it needed to fight Iraq not because of something that Iraq had clearly done, such as invading a neighboring nation, but because of something Iraq had at one time possessed and was possibly continuing to develop—weapons of mass destruction (WMD). ■

American tanks roll through the Saudi Arabian desert during the first Gulf War. American troops were sent to defend Saudi Arabia beginning in August 1990, when Saddam Hussein invaded Kuwait. This deployment of troops into Saudi Arabia was known as Operation Desert Shield.

BACKGROUND

TO WAR

In this most recent Gulf War, the fact that no definitive proof that Iraq had or was developing weapons of mass destruction was ever found virtually guaranteed that U.S. action would seem unjustified to many. Using this claim in the first place to justify such large-scale, unprecedented U.S. military action in the Middle East indicates just how important and frightening an issue weapons of mass destruction has become in the world. This is especially true with the growing fear that such weapons might wind up in the hands of terrorist groups or other organizations outside the control of any formal government structure. That Iraq should find itself at the center of such concerns is something that the Saddam Hussein era made quite probable.

THE COUNTRY AND PEOPLE OF IRAQ

In many ways, however, Iraq is an unlikely combatant for the United States. Iraq is not much larger than the state of California and is mostly landlocked. In area, the United States is twenty-one times larger than Iraq. The United States has a population of approximately 295 million; Iraq's population is about 25 million.

However, Iraq's location makes it strategically important. Iraq's borders include Turkey to the north, Iran to the east, Jordan and Syria to the west, and Kuwait, Saudi Arabia, and the Persian Gulf to the south. The country's major rivers are the Tigris and the Euphrates. Mesopotamia, the area between these two rivers, was known for centuries as the Fertile Crescent and "the cradle of civilization." Iraq also contains huge reserves of a substance without which modern civilization would be inconceivable—oil.

Most of the people of Iraq are Arabs, which means they speak Arabic. Almost all of Iraq's people are Muslims, followers of the religion of Islam, which uses Arabic

QUICK FACTS ABOUT IRAQ

Capital city: Baghdad

Other major cities: Basra, Mosul

Population: Approximately 25 million

Major rivers:

  Tigris: 1,150 miles (1,851 km)

  Euphrates: 1,460 miles (2,350 km)

Approximate geopolitical zones:

  Northern area: Mostly Kurdish

  Southern area: Mostly Shiite

  Middle area: Mostly Sunni

Average annual rainfall:

  4 to 7 inches (10 to 18 cm)

Average temperatures:

  Summer: 70°F to 110°F (21°C to 43°C)

  Winter: 50°F (10°C)

Major export: Oil

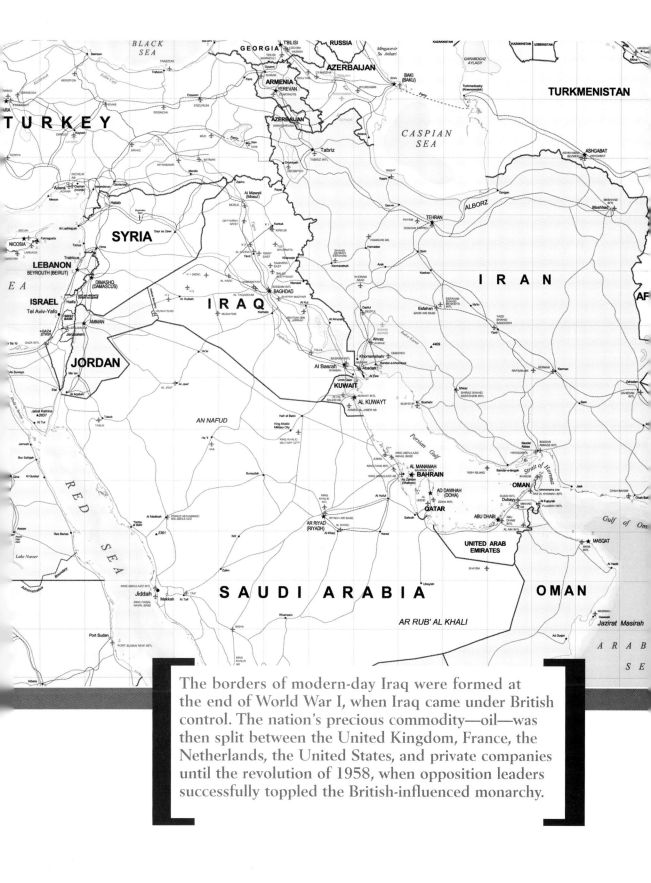

The borders of modern-day Iraq were formed at the end of World War I, when Iraq came under British control. The nation's precious commodity—oil—was then split between the United Kingdom, France, the Netherlands, the United States, and private companies until the revolution of 1958, when opposition leaders successfully toppled the British-influenced monarchy.

An Iraqi man passes an oil refinery on his donkey cart. In November 2003, Iraqi insurgents were using donkey carts to launch rockets against U.S. forces. This caused much difficulty for the Iraqis who depend on this mode of transportation for their livelihood, as they then came under serious inspections and were halted from travel.

as its language of worship. The Kurds, who live in northern Iraq and also in Iran, Armenia, Turkey, and Syria, are Iraq's largest minority group. They constitute 15 to 20 percent of Iraq's population. The Kurds are also mostly Muslim, but they are not Arabs; they speak their own language and regard their culture as being distinct from that of the Arabs.

The Arab Muslim population of Iraq is divided between two groups, the Sunnis and the Shia (or Shiites). Although both recognize the authority of Muhammad as the last and truest prophet of the one god (whom Muslims call Allah), they differ as to which of Muhammad's followers was the rightful inheritor of Islam's spiritual authority. These differences continue to the present day and reflect themselves in clashes over religious and political leadership. More than 60 percent of Iraq's Muslims are Shiites. The remainder, including Saddam Hussein, his family, and his strongest supporters, are Sunni. Sunnis are the minority group yet they have actually controlled political power in Iraq for years.

THE IMPORTANCE OF OIL

Although Iraq's written history dates back 300 centuries before the birth of Christ, Iraq has been a modern, independent nation less than 100 years. For four centuries, until the end of World War I in 1918, Iraq was part of the Ottoman Empire (present-day Turkey), like many of the modern Arab nations. After the war, the victorious European powers (England and France) divided most of the Ottoman Empire's former possessions between them. Iraq fell under British control, which lasted until 1932. In that year, Iraq finally gained its independence. Like the other Arab states, much of Iraq's history as an independent nation has resulted from the discovery that it possesses enormous reserves of oil, perhaps the modern world's most important resource—an estimated 10 percent of the world's total. This gave Iraq and the other oil-producing Arab nations an immediate source of potential great wealth and tremendous strategic importance in the world.

SADDAM HUSSEIN AND THE BAATH PARTY

Modern Iraq was a monarchy until 1958, when King Faisal II was overthrown and assassinated. After the rise and fall of a number of governments, most of them controlled by the military, the Baath Party took power in 1968. The party's leader at the time was Ahmad Hassan al-Bakr. Once in power, he surrounded himself with relatives and trusted associates from his hometown of Tikrit in northwest Iraq. Among these was Saddam Hussein, who had proved his loyalty by carrying out an assassination attempt on the head of the Iraqi government in 1959. By 1979, Hussein had been given

This is a photo of Saddam Hussein taken in 1980, shortly after Iraq began its war with Iran. Hussein first joined the Baath Party in 1956. By 1966, he had become the deputy secretary general of the party. He became president of Iraq in 1979.

control of most of the crucial government functions by an increasingly ill Bakr. When Bakr resigned from office that year, forty-two-year-old Hussein replaced him as president of Iraq.

Like Bakr and most of those whom he placed in high office, Hussein was a Sunni. The year he took office, an Islamic revolution in Iran took place. Iran is Iraq's larger, richer, more powerful, and more populous neighbor to the east. This revolution brought the Ayatollah Khomeini, an extremely revered, fundamentalist Shiite

Ayatollah Ruholla Khomeini is greeted by supporters in Tehran, Iran, in 1979, after years spent in exile. The title "ayatollah" means "supreme religious leader." Khomeini had returned from the Iraqi city of Najaf to lead the Islamic revolution in Iran. Iran became a symbol for Islamic fundamentalists throughout the Middle East because it successfully overturned a Westernized society for a pure Islamic state. Khomeini led this revolution until his death in 1989.

cleric, to power. Like Iraq, Iran is extremely rich in oil. Unlike Iraq, Iran's population is primarily Shiite. Also unlike Iraq, Iran had enjoyed an extremely close relationship with the United States. Indeed, before Khomeini came to power, Iran had been one of the United States' closest and most important allies in the Middle East. Finally, Iranians are Persians, not Arabs, with a long history of rivalry with the Arabs in the region. Iraq had spent long periods of its history under Persian rule.

All this presented the new ruler of Iraq with a major crisis. The Baath Party was secular, meaning it was not a religious organization. Many Muslims in Iraq were sympathetic to Khomeini's idea that government and law in Muslim nations should be organized according to Islamic law, with Muslim clerics holding the ultimate power. Khomeini's supporters were interested in spreading this idea outside Iran, and Iraq's

Shiites were an obvious source of support. Indeed, after being expelled from his native Iran in 1965, as a threat to the government, Khomeini had lived in exile in the Iraqi city of Najaf for thirteen years, during which he gained a loyal following among Iraq's Shiites. Threatened by his presence, Hussein had him expelled from Iraq in late 1978. As Iraq's new ruler, Hussein was very aware that the Shiites far outnumbered the Sunnis in his country, and these developments in Iran were thus a potential threat to his own power. He also saw an opportunity for Iraq

An Iranian soldier watches smoke billow from the burning oil refineries that were repeatedly bombed by Iraqi forces during the Iran-Iraq War in September 1980. The city where they are located, Abadan, Iran, was almost completely destroyed during the war. The United States and Soviet Union, as well as Egypt, Pakistan, and Saudi Arabia, sided with Iraq in the conflict, while Israel, South Africa, Taiwan, Libya, and Argentina sided with Iran.

to replace Iran as the most powerful nation in the region.

Hussein responded by going to war with Iran in 1980. Although the war lasted eight years, cost both countries millions of casualties, and ended in a stalemate, it was a decisive event in Hussein's regime. By the end of the war, an increasingly desperate Hussein had made Iraq the largest single purchaser of weapons and military equipment in the world. In that time, Iraq attempted to buy weapons from the Soviet Union, France, West Germany, China, Italy, Brazil, Poland, Czechoslovakia, and Egypt. Its largest supplier, however, was the United States, which sold Iraq $24 billion worth of military equipment between 1981 and 1985.

For the most part, sales of Iraqi oil paid for these weapons. The country had the revenue for such purchases, but the war really came at the expense of the Iraqi people.

Expenditures that might have gone toward the improvement of Iraqi society instead went to the war. By 1988, Hussein found himself

Iraqi soldiers wave white flags and surrender to allied forces in February 1991. Operation Desert Storm was an overwhelming attack against Iraq that consisted of 38 days of air attacks and 100 hours of ground fighting.

at the head of an increasingly demoralized and angry population. Large numbers of casualties had left even patriotic Iraqis tired of the war. Many Shiites immigrated to Iran and fought against Iraq. Iraq's Kurdish population used the turmoil as a chance to press again for its own long-sought independence. Faced with potential military catastrophe and unrest at home, Hussein became increasingly brutal in his rule, relying on the military and secret police to maintain power.

Hussein also quickly found himself on the wrong side of the world's only superpower, the United States. The United States was

angered by the events in Iran, its once crucial ally. The new Islamic rulers in Iran were openly hostile to the United States, therefore the United States had at least tacitly supported Iraq in the war with Iran, and had sold it an enormous amount of weapons. But when Hussein followed the Iran war disaster with Iraq's invasion of Kuwait in 1990, he immediately made an outright enemy of the United States, setting the stage for the events that would ultimately result in the second Gulf War and his downfall. ■

2

THE ARGUMENT

By the end of the first Gulf War, the world had ample demonstration that Saddam Hussein was certainly an erratic, untrustworthy, irresponsible, and cruel leader, one willing to use naked aggression and brute force, even against Iraq's people, to get what he wanted. His actions against Iraq's Kurdish population were one example. When the Kurds began to agitate for their own independence in the closing months of the Iran-Iraq War, Hussein diverted troops from the war effort to subdue the Kurds. The campaign was especially brutal. In a few months from 1987 to 1988, more than

100,000 Iraqi Kurds were killed, and several thousand Kurdish villages were destroyed. Of particular significance, in light of the world's later concerns, was that the Iraqi military used poison gas against the Kurds on at least some occasions. Earlier, Iraq had also used poison gas on the battlefield against Iran.

Hussein's conduct of the war against Kuwait provided another example. When he realized that his forces would not be able to hold Kuwait in the face of the U.S. intervention, he ordered Kuwait's oil fields torched. The result was an unprecedented environmental disaster and clear proof that Hussein had little regard for any chemical, biological, or environmental consequences of his actions.

By the end of the first Gulf War, the world also had much evidence of Hussein's interest in acquiring weapons, from virtually any source whatsoever. UN Resolution 687, which Hussein agreed to on April 3, 1991, and which functioned as the cease-fire agreement for the first Gulf War, reflected these concerns. According to its terms, Iraq would destroy or remove

The first Gulf War caused the worst environmental disaster in recent history. Over 600 oil wells were set on fire, and huge oil spills poured into the Persian Gulf. Wildlife such as green turtles and migratory birds perished. Pictures of oiled ducks, like the one above, became a symbol of the devastation to the ecosystem in this region.

The United Nations Security Council listened to the argument presented by U.S. Secretary of State Colin Powell on February 5, 2003, regarding Iraq's failure to disarm. He described the numerous ways Iraq had not complied with UN inspectors, continued to conceal weapons of mass destruction, and maintained ties with terrorists. Without the UN's support, the United States proceeded to go to war with Iraq the next month.

chemical and biological weapons and would agree not to acquire or develop nuclear weapons. Iraq also agreed to on-site inspections by a team from the United Nations.

JUSTIFICATION FOR WAR

During the year 2002, when the United States began to make the case that it needed to go to war with Iraq again, that argument was based almost solely on a single point: Hussein was developing weapons of mass destruction, and this made him an imminent danger to his neighbors in the Middle East, to the United States, and to the rest of the world. In other words, the justification for war was Hussein's alleged refusal to comply with the terms of UN Resolution 687 and other agreements regarding weapons control.

The unofficial borders of Kurdistan were erased at the end of World War I, when new nations were carved up by the Allied powers. Since then, 20 million Kurds have lived in the mountainous region where Turkey, Iran, and Iraq meet. Worldwide attention was brought to their plight in 1991, when media images captured the Kurds fleeing Hussein's Iraq for Turkey and Iran after the Gulf War. This is a photo of Kurdish refugees in Turkey at this time.

A CLOSER LOOK AT THE EFFECTS OF SANCTIONS ON IRAQ

While sanctions imposed by the UN did not seem to have much effect on Saddam Hussein, they hurt Iraqi citizens, most of all children. For example, the UN banned certain vaccines because they contained a small amount of a mustard derivative, which Iraq might use to make chemical weapons. By 1999, half of Iraq's livestock had died. Vaccines for preventing foot-and-mouth disease were not allowed because the material in the vaccines could be used to make biological weapons.

An Iraqi woman looks after her grandchild who is a leukemia patient in a Baghdad hospital. Radiation from depleted uranium munitions used by the United States and Great Britain when bombing Iraq is believed to be the cause of the rise in cancer after 1991.

Thousands of people died of malnutrition or from the inability to get needed medicines. The United States blew up Iraq's water treatment plants and sewage treatment plants along with electrical generating plants and communications centers during the Gulf War. Raw sewage contaminated Iraq's drinking water, but because of sanctions, Iraq could not purify its water. Iraq was not permitted to use chlorine, which could also be used in making weapons of mass destruction. Thousands of Iraqis, especially children, died from diarrhea, typhoid, and other diseases caused by contaminated water. Other causes of death included malnutrition or the inability to get needed medicines. It is estimated that more than 1.6 million deaths in Iraq were caused by the effects of UN sanctions.

As Paul Wolfowitz, the U.S. deputy secretary of defense explained in an interview published in the May 2003 issue of *Vanity Fair* magazine, "We settled on the one issue that everyone could agree on, which was weapons of mass destruction as the core reason" for going to war.

As of the middle of 2004, the United States, by then present in all of Iraq, had yet to present convincing evidence that Iraq had, in fact, the capability of producing WMD in any significant capacity. This failure to find WMD was what made the war so controversial around the world. Debate raged as to whether the administration of President George W. Bush had simply been mistaken about Hussein's weapons programs or whether it had intentionally misled the American people and U.S. allies about what it knew about Hussein and WMD.

That question will probably not be answered for years. What can be more immediately understood is why even the possibility that Hussein was developing WMD should have suddenly seemed such an immediate threat in the first years of the twenty-first century that it required an invasion of Iraq. After all, UN Resolution 687 had been signed in 1991. Eleven years had passed in which Hussein had hindered, objected to, and at times refused to allow UN inspections. Why did the crisis become so acute in 2002 and 2003?

> "We settled on the one issue that everyone could agree on, which was weapons of mass destruction."
>
> *Paul Wolfowitz*

Part of the explanation lay simply in changes in government in the United States. As previously mentioned, President George H. W. Bush had acted to drive Iraqi forces from Kuwait, but he was not willing to invade Iraq itself to remove Hussein. In 1992, Bush was defeated in his bid for reelection to the presidency by Bill Clinton. The Clinton administration preferred to deal with Iraq and the WMD issue by relying on UN inspections of alleged Iraqi weapons sites, despite Hussein's frequent refusal to cooperate. On certain occasions of Hussein's outright defiance of the UN, Clinton ordered U.S. bombing raids as a sign of U.S. displeasure and made other threatening military gestures in the region, but for the most part relied on UN economic sanctions against Iraq to force compliance.

Under the terms of these sanctions, the nations of the world were forbidden to conduct normal trade with Iraq. The idea was to leave Iraq economically isolated, especially by preventing it from selling its oil on the world market, thereby forcing it to cooperate with the UN. The sanctions greatly damaged the Iraqi economy, contributing to the death (according to the UN) of an estimated 500,000 Iraqi children under the age of five by denying them adequate nutrition, health care, and hygiene. Nonetheless, Hussein continued his policy of non-cooperation.

After 1998, Iraq essentially refused to allow any further UN inspections. However, UN inspectors have stated that by that point, 90 to 95 percent of any Iraqi WMD programs had already been dismantled.

SEPTEMBER 11, 2001

In January 2001, Clinton was succeeded as president of the United States by George W. Bush, the son of the president who had directed the first Gulf War. The new President Bush surrounded himself in office with many people who had served and advised his father. Many of these advisers had come to believe that it had been a mistake not to invade Iraq and depose Hussein in 1991. Hussein's alleged development of WMD in the years since seemed only to strengthen this argument. This alone would almost certainly have brought about a more aggressive U.S. policy toward Iraq. However, it was the events of September 11, 2001, that gave the issue of Iraq and WMD an entirely new sense of urgency.

On that day, terrorists associated with the Islamic fundamentalist terrorist group Al Qaeda hijacked four passenger jets in the United States and intentionally crashed them into the Pentagon building outside Washington, D.C., and into the Twin Towers of the World Trade Center in New York City, resulting in a huge loss of life and tremendous economic damage. The fourth plane crashed into the countryside of western Pennsylvania, after the passengers struggled with the hijackers. It was the bloodiest day in U.S. history since the U.S. Civil War (1861–1865), and it marked the first significant attack by a foreign power on the U.S. mainland since the War of 1812.

Colin Powell, the U.S. secretary of state is shown on a screen in Times Square in New York City, as he speaks to the UN Security Council on February 5, 2003. Powell's argument for action against Iraq included spy satellite images, telephone intercepts, and statements from Iraqi defectors as proof of a suspected weapons program. The UN Security Council's response was one of deep division: Great Britain became the United States' staunchest ally, while France maintained that war should be the last resort. Iraq's UN ambassador called Powell's presentation "utterly unrelated to the truth."

For the first time, Americans were forced to realize that terrorism was not just a foreign problem, and that the United States itself was vulnerable to a major terrorist attack. It also made Americans more aware, and more fearful, of the danger of any kind of foreign attack, which made the prospect of WMD in the hands of an enemy of the United States, such as Saddam Hussein, more frightening.

Although at this point in history only a handful of governments have shown the capability of developing WMD, the possibility that such weapons could somehow be passed from a government to a terrorist group began to seem much more realistic and terrifying. After all, Al Qaeda had centered its operations in Afghanistan with the close cooperation of the government there. What was to prevent someone like Hussein from passing WMD to a terrorist group that opposed the United States? With such reasoning, President Bush argued that an invasion of Iraq was a necessary part of the "War on Terror" that he had declared in the aftermath of the September 11 attacks, even though there was very little real evidence that Hussein had any close connections with Al Qaeda or any ability to provide it with WMD. ■

The Tuwaitha Nuclear Facility was Iraq's largest nuclear complex, located about 30 miles (50 km) outside of Baghdad. It is pictured here shortly after the fall of Saddam Hussein in June 2003. The complex suffered extensive damage from U.S. bombing during the first Gulf War. Though what remained of its uranium materials had been accounted for in 2002, there were concerns that parts of the facility had been reconstructed and a nuclear program had resumed.

IRAQ AND NUCLEAR WEAPONS

3

A 2002 White House document defined WMD as "nuclear, biological, and chemical weapons in the possession of hostile states and terrorists." For most people, the greatest fear regarding Iraq and WMD was the idea that Iraq was developing a nuclear weapons program.

Nuclear and atomic weapons are the deadliest of weapons of mass destruction. The United States was the first to develop nuclear weapons, and it remains the only nation to use them against another nation. That action occurred in August 1945, when the United States dropped atomic bombs on the Japanese cities of Hiroshima and Nagasaki to bring about the end of World War II (1939–1945).

The devastation to those cities was greater than anything the world had seen. Huge sections of both cities were flattened, and the immediate number of deaths was somewhere between 100,000 and 120,000 people. Thousands more people died in the months and years to come as a result of exposure to the radiation from the blast. Indeed, the damaging effects of radiation from nuclear weapons make them a type of chemical weapon as well.

In the years since, despite various international efforts to control the proliferation of nuclear weapons, several nations besides the United States have developed their own weapons. Although developing a capable nuclear weapons system is enormously difficult and expensive, possession of nuclear weapons is often seen as a sign that a nation has become a true military power, secure from attack by other nations, and worthy of respect and fear from the rest of the world. Today, besides the United States, Russia, France, Great Britain, and China possess nuclear weapons and are "allowed" to do so by international treaty (the Nuclear Non-Proliferation Treaty of 1968). India, Pakistan, and Israel have developed nuclear weapons outside of any international treaty agreement. North Korea is currently pursuing nuclear capabilities, and Iran is believed to be. The United States has the world's largest nuclear arsenal.

THE IRAQI PROGRAM

There is no doubt that Iraq has long had an interest in developing nuclear weapons. According to Khidhir Hamza, an Iraqi nuclear scientist who defected to the United States in 1994, Iraq began working on developing nuclear weapons as early as 1971, years before Hussein came to power.

A nuclear weapon first needs a critical mass of fissile material, uranium 235 or plutonium. These heavy metals are necessary to fuel a first-generation fission bomb. Production of fuel is the most difficult part of making a nuclear bomb. For one thing, scientists must separate U-235 from the more abundant U-238 isotopes. This process is called enrichment.

Iraqi scientists apparently learned about enrichment from the Manhattan Project, which was the code name for the secret U.S. effort to develop an atomic bomb during World War II. Hamza says he found declassified Manhattan Project reports about enrichment on the shelves of Iraq's Atomic Energy Commission. These reports were apparently a gift from the United States at the time that Iraq was launching its civilian atomic energy project in 1956.

In 1974, Iraq bought a nuclear reactor from France. The Iraqis called the reactor Tammuz I and established it outside Baghdad. In June 1981, Israel, which has always opposed the development of nuclear power by any of its Arab enemies, destroyed Tammuz I with a surprise air raid. (With the exception of Egypt and Jordan, the Arab nations of the Middle East have been in an unending declared state of war with Israel since the establishment of Israel as an independent nation in 1948.)

According to Hamza, Iraq renewed its pursuit of nuclear weapons during the

Dr. Khidhir Hamza is pictured here being sworn in during a hearing of a U.S. congressional committee where he testified about Iraq's nuclear program on September 25, 2002. At the time, Congress was looking into Iraq's nuclear capabilities and trying to determine if U.S. intervention was necessary.

IRAQ'S MISSILE PROGRAM

The following list, obtained from the Federation of American Scientists and BBC News Online from November 18, 2002, lists the Scud-type missile programs pursued by Iraq under Saddam Hussein. Of these, only the al-Hussein is known to have achieved full operational capacity. Sixty al-Husseins were fired at Israel and Saudi Arabia during the first Gulf War, with extremely limited impact. There is no evidence, for example, that the al-Abbas was ever test fired more than once or that it achieved operational capacity.

Missile Range

al-Hussein

375 miles (600 km)

al-Hijarah

470 miles (750 km)

al-Abbas

560 miles (900 km)

Iraq's Scud ballistic missiles

These modified Soviet-era missiles are considered old-fashioned technology, but capable of delivering chemical or biological weapons.

Guidance system: Crude gyroscope system

Impact fuse

Warhead

Missile range
375 mi. (600 km)
■ Hits within 1 to 2 miles of target

Baghdad

Launch
From heavy mobile launchers

Past use
Iran-Iraq war (1980-88)   500 launched

Gulf War (1991)   90 launched

■ Iraq believed to have about 20 Scuds left

Liquid fuel tank

Oxidizer tank

Length
41 ft. (13 m)

Diameter
35 in. (89 cm)

Rocket motor
After rocket motor stops firing, missile coasts unguided toward target

Source: BBC, Federation of American Scientists, U.S. Defense Dept., KRT Photo Service
Graphic: Todd Lindeman, Judy Treible
© 2003 KRT

This profile shows Iraq's missile capability and a typical mobile launcher obtained from the Soviet Union that was capable of delivering chemical or biological weapons.

Iran-Iraq War with some degree of success. It did manage to import enough enriched uranium to run Tammuz I, and some of that supply remained even after the Israeli raid. Iraq also had some success in developing its own uranium mine, although it is doubtful that it ever has had the technology to enrich that uranium. Hamza claims that between 1987 and 1990, Iraq spent $10 million on developing nuclear weapons. This is actually a very small amount of what is needed for such a program, and the best evidence is that Iraq made very little progress in developing nuclear weapons after the first Gulf War and the beginning of the 2002 UN inspections.

Despite Hussein's opposition to UN inspections, the International Atomic Energy Agency (IAEA), which is the international agency entrusted by the UN with responsibility for nuclear issues, believed that all of the fissile material that Iraq could have used to make nuclear weapons had been removed, although it acknowledged that it could not give an absolute guarantee. The fact that fears of an Iraqi nuclear capability played a part in the U.S. decision to go to war is indicated by President Bush's statement during a speech given on January 28, 2003, that Iraq had attempted to buy significant portions of uranium from the African nation of Niger. The president's statement was later shown to be based on falsified documents. Despite that and several other similar statements made by President Bush and members of his administration, the IAEA has consistently maintained that there is no evidence of a viable nuclear weapons program in Iraq.

MISSILES

Missile capability is an important consideration in analyzing any country's potential for developing WMD. Missiles are an essential part of any WMD program because in the absence of an extremely powerful air force—and at present the United States has the most powerful one—ballistic missiles are the most likely means by which a nuclear weapon could be delivered against the United States or another enemy. A ballistic missile is a self-propelled rocket that is launched through the air in a guided, arched trajectory carrying a "payload" of explosive

Here, Scud missiles are being bull-dozed in 1991, under the supervision of UNSCOM inspectors at an Iraqi military camp. UNSCOM was a special commission created by the UN Security Council to inspect Iraq's nuclear, chemical, and biological weapon capabilities. Iraq was ordered to destroy all of its Scud missiles with a range greater than 90 miles (150 km) and UNSCOM inspectors were to be allowed access to all such facilities to ensure this had been carried out.

weapons. The most sophisticated missiles can travel at speeds of up to 15,000 miles per hour (24,140 kilometers per hour), can be launched from submarines, can travel from continent to continent, and can carry nuclear warheads. Only the United States, Russia, France, Great Britain, and China have the capacity thus far to create such sophisticated ballistic missiles.

A U.S. marine radiation expert checks radiation levels with a detector on equipment outside the Tuwaitha Nuclear Facility in June 2003. The facility had been looted following the topple of Saddam Hussein's regime. Although the CIA had encouraged inspectors in 2002 to search this facility, the inspectors came up empty-handed. Radiation was detected in recent tests, but it was more than likely from a legitimate source of radioactive material Iraqi scientists are allowed to have.

Iraq has never come close to developing such sophisticated ballistic weapons systems. Indeed, UN Resolution 687 said that Iraq must destroy, remove, and quit research on ballistic missiles with a range greater than 90 miles (150 km). Most of Iraq's missiles (Scuds) were imported from the Soviet Union and were exhausted during the war with Iran. Although

33

Iraq fired several Scud missiles at Israel and Saudi Arabia during the first Gulf War, the missiles did little damage.

Iraq under Hussein showed persistent interest in upgrading its missile systems, but there is no evidence that it enjoyed any great success. Various ambitious projects were pursued, but according to UN inspection teams and the Federation of American Scientists, a U.S. nuclear watchdog group, the entire Iraqi missile inventory at the time of the second Gulf War consisted of, at best, six to fifty Scud-like missiles. These missiles would have had a maximum range of 375 miles (600 km) if operational, which inspectors concluded was exceedingly unlikely. Operational missiles with such a range could pose a threat to Iraq's neighbors but would clearly be of no danger to the United States. ■

UN inspectors arrive with bags and testing equipment at a phosphate plant in Iraq on January 7, 2003. The inspectors used helicopters for travel and aerial inspections. It had been four years since inspections had been carried out. Their efforts resumed in November 2002, and continued steadily into January 2003, in a search for chemical, biological, and nuclear weapons that Iraq continued to deny that it had. The inspectors' report of their findings was due to the UN Security Council on January 27, 2003.

IRAQ AND CHEMICAL WEAPONS

Of all the arguments regarding Iraq's possession of WMD, those regarding chemical weapons probably carry the most weight. Hussein had used chemical weapons before, in the war against Iran and against the Kurds, and there were signs that he intended to maintain Iraq's ability to conduct chemical warfare.

WHAT ARE CHEMICAL WEAPONS?

Chemical weaponry is the intentional use of poisonous substances to cause injury or death. The Geneva Protocol of 1925, an international agreement, bans the use of asphyxiating, poisonous, or other gases in warfare. It does not, however, ban the production or stockpiling of such weapons. The United States finally ratified the Geneva Protocol in 1975. In 1997, the United States ratified the Chemical Weapons Convention (CWC), which complements the Geneva Protocol. The CWC does ban the production and stockpiling of chemical weapons. It committed those who signed it to dismantling chemical weapons and their production facilities by 2007. Iraq did not sign this treaty.

The most common chemical weapons include mustard gas and the nerve agents tabun, sarin, and VX. Mustard gas, which smells like garlic or mustard, can blister the skin and burn the eyes and lungs. Those who suffer from intense exposure to mustard gas may die from lung damage. Germany used mustard gas in World War I; Japan used it in World War II.

Nerve agents are even more deadly. They attack the central nervous system by affecting the enzymes necessary for transmitting "messages" from nerves to muscles, producing muscle spasms and paralysis soon after exposure. VX is the most toxic of the nerve gases.

IRAQ'S POSSESSION OF MUSTARD GAS

Iraq began research on mustard gas (dichloroethyl sulphide) in the 1970s and had produced it by the 1980s. By 1983, the U.S. government was aware that Iraq had used mustard gas against Iran and that Hussein was desperate to upgrade Iraq's stock of weapons, including chemical agents. Although officially neutral in the Iran-Iraq War, internal U.S. policy was to ensure that Iraq was not defeated by Iran and that the war did not interfere with the flow of oil from the Persian Gulf. To that end, the administration of U.S. president Ronald Reagan offered several gentle public condemnations of Iraqi use of chemical weapons and even intervened at least once to prevent

A UN worker in a protective suit punctures a 122-millimeter sarin rocket during an October 1991 inspection in Iraq. From June 1992 to June 1994, a special UN commission destroyed 70 tons of this nerve agent in Iraq. By the time UNSCOM left Iraq in 1998, it had incapacitated a large portion of Iraq's chemical weapon potential.

the sale of necessary chemical weapons ingredients by a U.S. company to Iraq for that purpose. At the time, the United States was putting much greater effort into discouraging international arms sales to Iran.

NERVE AGENTS: TABUN, SARIN, AND VX GASES

Originally developed to kill insects and other pests, nerve agents can also kill people. Tabun and sarin are so-called G-series agents. Both were developed in Germany in the 1930s, during the regime of the Nazi dictator Adolf Hitler.

V-series agents are more powerful than G-series agents. VX gas is an example of a V-series agent. If absorbed through the skin, VX is 2,000 times more toxic than mustard gas. Great Britain developed VX in the

A UN inspector takes a sample of a nerve agent from a container during UNSCOM's 1991 inspections. The CIA believed that gaps in Iraq's accounting and capabilities up until the U.S. invasion of 2003 pointed to a strong chemical weapons program. In 1998, the UN found that Iraq had at one time overstated its chemical weapons stockpile.

early 1950s, and exchanged the formula with the United States in return for nuclear secrets.

Nerve agents can be dispersed as a spray of liquid or as a cloud of vapor. They can enter the body through the skin, eyes, or lungs. Within minutes of inhalation, nerve agents can attack the nervous system; they are likely to cause paralysis, respiratory failure, and death.

By 1984, Iraq had developed the capability to produce tabun, sarin, and VX. Most of these chemical weapons, along with mustard gas, were produced at what was known as the Muthanna State Establishment, Iraq's primary production, testing, storing, and filling facility for chemical weapons. Sole authority for the use of such weapons rested with Hussein. Requests for the use of chemical weapons could be made by the general staff of the Iraqi military or by commanders in the field, but Hussein had to personally approve all such requests.

QUICK FACTS ABOUT CHEMICAL AND BIOLOGICAL WARFARE

- Chemical weapons are more expensive to make than biological weapons.
- Chemical weapons are generally more stable than biological weapons.
- Chemical weapons are generally easier to make.
- Chemical weapons are usually more predictable in warfare.
- Chemical weapons require larger facilities to produce and store.

BOTH:

- Injure and kill.
- Cause pollution to land and water.
- Harm living things (rather than structures).
- Are relatively inexpensive to produce.
- Can be made in facilities that make commercial products, such as insecticides.
- Can have various modes of delivery, such as cruise missiles, or common vehicles, such as cars and trucks.

CHEMICAL ALI AND THE KURDS

In all likelihood, Iraq used both mustard gas and nerve agents against Iran on the battlefield. Its most lethal use, however, was against Iraq's Kurdish population. By the end of the Iran-Iraq War, Kurds constituted about 20

percent of the Iraqi population and were significant minorities in Iran, Syria, Turkey, and Armenia. In all of these countries, the Kurds considered themselves a distinct cultural and national group and had long been attempting to gain their independence, often with violent opposition by the ruling powers. By 1987, much of Iraq's Kurdish population was in open revolt against Hussein. The Kurds were encouraged by Iran, which hinted that if the Kurds helped it defeat Iraq, it would grant them independence.

Hussein responded brutally. He appointed his cousin Ali Hassan al-Majid as the head of the Iraqi government in Iraq's northern zone, where the Kurdish population was centered. There, Majid earned the nicknames "Chemical Ali" and the "Butcher of Kurdistan" for his suppression of

Mustard gas-filled bombs are spread across the ground during a UNSCOM inspection in 1991. Mustard gas had been used in attacks against Iranians and Kurds, killing thousands between 1983 and 1988. Inset: Lieutenant General Ali Hassan al-Majid, better known as Chemical Ali, attends a military parade in Baghdad with Saddam Hussein in 2000. Ali, Hussein's cousin, allegedly carried out the chemical attacks on the Kurds in 1988. He was taken into U.S. custody in August 2003.

Local Iraqis led soldiers to a secret underground bunker at Chemical Ali's intelligence headquarters in April 2003. Frogmen, as the army divers are called, explored water in the bunker, initially setting off a bio-chemical alert, but all tests eventually proved negative for traces of biological and chemical weapons.

the Kurdish uprising. Rural Kurds were gathered into concentration camps. Several thousand villages were destroyed, and 100,000 Kurds were killed.

The most notorious attack was directed against the Kurdish town of Halabja. For three days in March 1988, Iraqi forces used mustard gas, sarin, tabun, and possibly VX against the town. More than 5,000 Halabja Kurds were killed instantly. Countless survivors were burned and scarred by mustard gas, while birth defects were common in the children of survivors who had been exposed to the nerve agents. At least forty other similar attacks on Kurdish villages took place at the time. Following the first Gulf War, Majid was ordered by Hussein to

A pile of corn was inspected on a private farm during weapons inspections by a UN worker on January 17, 2003. By this time, UN inspectors were drawing close to their deadline of reporting their findings to the UN Security Council but had wanted to extend the deadline to continue their search in an effort to avoid war.

quell a Shiite rebellion by the so-called marsh Arabs in southern Iraq. Majid used similarly ruthless methods to subdue the uprising.

A CONTINUING CAPABILITY?

All told, Iraq used an estimated 3,000 tons of chemical warfare agents in its war against Iran and the Kurds. These "weaponized forms" of chemicals were delivered by conventional artillery, warheads on Scud missiles, and in bombs dropped from planes. Although Iraq did not use chemical weapons with any success in the Gulf War, the UN clearly had good reason for including chemical weapons in the terms of UN Resolution 687. The same year that it agreed to UN Resolution 687, Iraq admitted to UN inspectors that it had produced almost 4,000 tons of chemical weapons between 1982 and 1990, along with more than 100,000 artillery shells, bombs, warheads, and other munitions capable of being filled with chemical weapons.

Despite Hussein's generally resistant attitude regarding UN inspections, by 1998, the UN Special Commission (UNSCOM) appointed to deal with Iraq on weapons issues declared that it could account for the destruction of the great majority of Iraq's chemical weapons arsenal. That same year, Iraq announced that it had resolved all of its remaining issues with UNSCOM and that it would no longer allow UN inspections. Although the United States and other nations were extremely skeptical about Iraq's statements, when UN inspections resumed in 2002, they found no significant evidence of a new Iraqi buildup of chemical weapons.

In its arguments in favor of invading Iraq, the Bush administration made several statements insisting that Iraq's chemical weapons still posed a threat. However, after the U.S. invasion of the country, no significant stockpiles or chemical weapons productions facilities were found. As was the case with nuclear weapons, the Iraqis also apparently had at no time any weapons delivery systems—missiles, rockets, bombs, or planes—capable of delivering a chemical weapon attack against the United States. And Iraq did not use chemical weapons in resisting the U.S. invasion, which might be seen as an indication that it did not possess such weapons. ■

This photo, released by the CIA, shows vials that contain single-cell proteins and biopesticides as well as other agents that could be used to produce biological weapons. Recovered from the home of an Iraqi scientist, they were consistent with information the CIA had already obtained. However, the team led by David Kay in Iraq recovered no such equipment and alleged hidden stockpiles in its extensive search from November 2002 to January 2003.

IRAQ AND
BIOLOGICAL
WEAPONS

Although they are classified as weapons of mass destruction **WEAPONS** and probably engender as much fear as chemical weapons, biological weapons have never been employed with any great degree of success, if by "success" one means deadly effect. Even so, recent years have witnessed a seeming increase in concern over the possibility that biological weapons might be used by a government or terrorist group. And the fear that Hussein might be developing such weapons played a role in the U.S. decision to pursue the Iraq war.

Ironically, both the United States and Iraq had signed the Biological and Toxin Weapons Convention (BTWC) treaty in 1972, but neither adhered to it. Under Hussein, Iraq ultimately failed to ratify the treaty, and under President George W. Bush, the United States pulled out of the treaty. The BTWC prohibits the development, production, stockpiling, or acquisition of biological agents or toxins of types and in quantities that have no justification for preventive, protective, or peaceful purposes. Both Bush and Hussein, however, thought that the methods of enforcement of the treaty, such as spot inspections by international inspectors, would be too intrusive.

WHAT IS BIOLOGICAL WARFARE?

Biological warfare is the intentional use of microorganisms to cause disease or death. Biological agents most likely to be used as weapons include bacteria, viruses, and toxins.

Some biological agents are more lethal than others. Some have a higher potential for use as weapons of mass destruction. Therefore, the Centers for Disease Control and Prevention (CDC) developed categories of risk (A, B, and C). Agents in category A have the highest potential to cause mass casualties. Examples of agents in the A category include anthrax, smallpox, and botulinum toxin.

A BACTERIUM: ANTHRAX

Of the A category agents, the one most commonly investigated for use as a weapon of mass destruction is anthrax, which is caused by the bacterium *Bacillus anthracis*. Most often a disease that infects animals, particularly cattle and sheep, anthrax can also infect humans, primarily through contact with an infected animal or with products from an infected animal, such as wool or meat. Infection in humans begins when spores enter the body through inhalation, ingestion, or contact with a break in the skin.

U.S. Secretary of State Colin Powell presents the UN with a vial of an unknown substance during his presentation to the UN Security Council on February 5, 2003. In his argument, he compared the amount of the contents inside the vial, a teaspoon, to the amount of anthrax found in the envelopes sent to congressional offices in the 2001 anthrax attacks.

Inhalation anthrax is the most dangerous form of the disease and the form most likely to be used as a weapon. Humans do not transmit anthrax to others; a person must be exposed to the bacteria. The incubation period for inhalation anthrax can vary from two days to six weeks with an average of approximately ten days. Symptoms include chills and fever, fatigue, cough, shortness of breath, and nausea and vomiting, and may progress until the infected person dies. If the infection is detected early enough, the person infected with anthrax may be treated with antibiotics, which is often, but not always, successful. The U.S. military has made an anthrax vaccine available for troops sent to the Persian Gulf region, but its effectiveness is uncertain and has even been alleged to cause other medical conditions.

Because anthrax spores are so small—thousands of spores can fit on the head of a pin— it has long been fascinating for weapons developers. U.S. Air Force medical officer Lieutenant-Colonel Robert Kadlec says that 220 pounds (100 kilograms) of anthrax dropped on a city the size

of Washington, D.C., could kill between 1 and 3 million people. Other experts, however, say that such fears are overblown. They point out that anthrax spores deteriorate upon contact with open air and that weapons-grade anthrax is exceedingly difficult to refine.

There is no doubt, however, that anthrax can be deadly. In September 2001, shortly after the terrorist attacks on the World Trade Center and the Pentagon, *Bacillus anthracis* spores sent via the U.S. mail infected

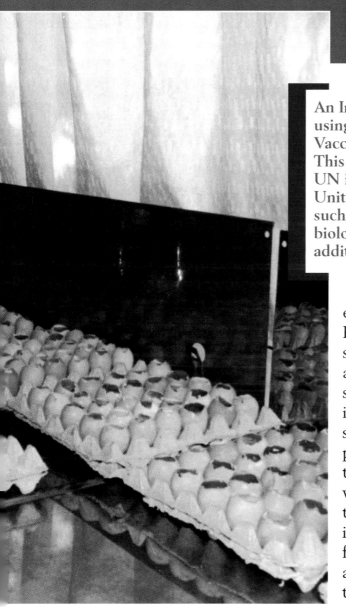

An Iraqi scientist conducts vaccine testing using eggs at the Amiriyah Serum and Vaccine Institute in Abu Ghraib, Iraq. This photo was taken during the 1998 UN inspections. The United States and United Nations feared that institutes such as this were dual use, with secret biological weapons being produced in addition to vaccines.

eleven people in the United States. Five of those infected died. Although scientists later discovered that the anthrax in the letters came from a strain of the germ known to originate in U.S. laboratories, the incident only served to aggravate the already rampant fear of what could happen if terrorists were to gain access to weapons of mass destruction. Twenty-two years earlier, an anthrax epidemic in Sverdlovsk, in the Soviet Union, following the accidental release of anthrax spores from a weapons factory there, had similarly demonstrated the spores' deadly potential.

IRAQ AND BIOLOGICAL WEAPONS

Iraq began to seriously pursue the production of biological weapons in 1985. Most of the research was done at so-called dual-use facilities, where more benign biological research was also pursued. Such dual-use facilities included the al-Dawrah Foot-and-Mouth Vaccine Institute and the Amiriyah Serum and Vaccine Institute. In 1988, Iraq

TEN NATIONS AND THEIR CURRENT WMD STANDINGS

The following list of nations, in order of their military expenditures, was compiled from the Nuclear Threat Initiative (NTI) and the Carnegie Endowment for International Peace. Both organizations are concerned with providing public access to the latest information in international policies concerning threats to world peace.

Nation	Nuclear	Chemical	Biological	Military Expenditure
United States	10,600+	Estimated at 30,000 metric tons	Research in biodefense	$420 billion
China	400 approx.	Suspected	Suspected	$50 billion
France	350 warheads	0	0	$46.8 billion
United Kingdom	200 warheads	0	Strong biodefense only	$31.8 billion (approx.)
Russia	20,000 approx.	Largest in world at 40,000 metric tons	Active test sites remain	$22.4 billion
India	529 to 871 kg	Weapon-grade plutonium (for 45 to 95 weapons)	1,000 tons suspected	$10.2 billion
Israel	100 to 200	Offensive program suspected	Offensive program suspected	$9.4 billion
Pakistan	1,279 to 1,764 kg highly enriched uranium (for 30 to 55 fission bombs)	Suspected	Suspected	$3.2 billion
North Korea	Fissile material only	Produces 4,500 tons	Suspected	N/A
Iran	Suspected	Suspected	Suspected	N/A

From www.nti.org and www.ceip.org/nonprolif/map

tested biological agents on various animals, including dogs, monkeys, sheep, and donkeys. Researchers sprayed germ aerosols near the animals to see which ones died first and how they died.

When, in April 1991, Iraq agreed to UN Resolution 687 and the resulting supervision and inspections by UNSCOM and the IAEA, it admitted to having a program of biological weapons research. However, the Hussein government insisted that the program was for defense purposes only.

Four years later, following the defection of Hussein Kamel, who was Hussein's son-in-law and the director of Iraq's military industries, Iraq admitted that between 1988 and 1991, it had conducted testing of biological weapons, including those that made use of the organisms that cause anthrax and botulism. It claimed that its primary biological weapons facility, the laboratory of the Technical Research Center at Salman Pak, had been destroyed by U.S. forces during the Gulf War. Iraq went on to claim that it had destroyed almost 3,400 gallons (13,000 liters) of biological weapons agents in compliance with UN Resolution 687. UNSCOM inspectors concluded, however, that Iraq had probably produced as

Hussein Kamel provided a wealth of information to UNSCOM about Iraq's WMD, including the fact that Iraq had destroyed much of its program after the Gulf War. In 1996, Kamel and his family were convinced to return to Iraq, only for Kamel to be denounced as a traitor, ordered to divorce his wife, and finally killed by Iraqi security forces.

much as four times the amount of biological weapons material than it had admitted to producing. In 1996, UNSCOM destroyed Iraq's main biological weapons facility at al-Hakam, 37 miles (60 km) southwest of Baghdad, yet the inspectors conceded that it was difficult to estimate how much, if any, biological weapons material Iraq might still have available.

Such uncertainty led the Bush administration to emphasize the danger posed by Hussein's possible possession of biological weapons. For example, in a speech given in October 2002, President Bush emphasized that UNSCOM "inspectors concluded that Iraq had likely produced two to four times" the amount it had previously admitted to. "This is a massive stockpile of biological weapons," Bush continued, "that has never been accounted for and is capable of killing millions." However, there is no indication that Iraq was anywhere near capable of producing an authentic weapon of mass destruction from whatever anthrax it did still possess.

> "This is a massive stockpile of biological weapons that has never been accounted for and is capable of killing millions."
>
> *President George W. Bush*

Indeed, there was the fear that Iraq had large stores of anthrax and the dangerous botulinum toxin, and had even conducted experiments with the virus that causes small-pox, the most deadly infectious disease in human history. Yet U.S. forces in Iraq after March 2003 found no evidence that Iraq possessed any significant biological weapons capability. As is the case with nuclear and chemical weapons, there was little evidence that Iraq did in fact possess weapons of mass destruction in the form of biological agents at the time of the U.S. invasion. On January 23, 2004, chief weapons-inspector David Kay resigned. In an interview with Reuters, reported by the *New York Times*, Kay said he thought Iraq had secret weapons at the end of the 1991 Gulf War, but that UN inspections and Iraq's own decisions "got rid of them." When asked if he believed that Iraq did not have stock-piles of chemical and biological weapons at the beginning of the second U.S. war with Iraq, Kay said, "That is correct."

CONCLUSION: THE ISG REPORT

In October 2004, Charles Duelfer, who replaced David Kay as chief weapons inspector, presented a report to Congress on behalf of his team, the Iraq Survey Group (ISG). The report concluded that Iraq had no nuclear, chemical, or biological weapons capability at the time of the recent U.S. invasion. The report stated that Hussein ended Iraq's nuclear and chemical programs in 1991 and that there was no evidence that they had been restarted. Iraq's last secret factory, a biological weapons plant, was destroyed in 1996. The report did state, however, that Hussein intended to resume

David Kay, the former top U.S. weapons inspector of Iraq, is pictured here testifying before the U.S. Senate Armed Services Committee in Washington, D.C., in January 2004. Kay resigned from his CIA job following his team's effort in Iraq to find weapons of mass destruction, citing that not enough resources had been allocated to complete the job. He felt that the intelligence community had relied too heavily on the reports from defectors, but in truth, everyone had been wrong about Iraq's WMD program.

production when UN sanctions were lifted. Critics of the recent U.S. invasion see this report as proof that Iraq did not pose an imminent threat and that U.S. military action was not justified. According to the Bush administration, the report is proof of Hussein's intentions and justifies the decision to go to war. Moreover, President Bush argues that the world is better off without Saddam Hussein. The U.S. argument for war was based almost solely, at least in public, on Hussein's possession of weapons of mass destruction, not on the fact that he was a brutal and dangerous leader. So as it is turning out that Iraq did not possess such weapons, then what happens to that justification for war? Regardless of how one answers that question, there is no doubt that there is good cause for the fear that weapons of mass destruction engender, and that the weapons will continue to be a major issue in determining power, peace, and prosperity in the world well into the future. ■

[GLOSSARY]

Arabs The approximately 256 million people who use the Arabic language. Iraqis, except for the Kurds, are Arabs.

Ayatollah Ruholla Khomeini The supreme religious leader of Iran from 1979 until his death in 1989.

Baath Party The Arab Baath Socialist Resurrection Party formed by two Syrian university students in 1947. The party offers a Socialist vision, bridging differences among those who speak Arabic.

Baghdad The capital city of Iraq.

ballistic missile A missile that travels unguided to its target when launched.

biological weapons Microorganisms used to cause disease or death in large number of people.

chemical weapons Poisonous substances intentionally used to cause injury and death.

IAEA (International Atomic Energy Agency) The agency created by the UN in 1957 to monitor civilian uses of nuclear energy as well as to monitor the Nuclear Non-Proliferation Treaty.

Islam The religion founded by the prophet Muhammad. The word means "submission" (to the will of a single God).

Kurds A non-Arab minority group that lives in several countries, including Iraq. The Kurds desire an independent territory.

Mesopotamia A Greek word that means "land between the rivers," specifically the Tigris and the Euphrates. The site of the early civilization of Iraq.

Muhammad Founder of Islam, born in Mecca in what is now Saudi Arabia in approximately 570.

Muslim A person who is a follower of the Islamic religion.

nuclear weapons Explosive devices that rely on the splitting or combining of atomic nuclei to release destructive energy.

Ottoman Turks One of the greatest single world powers during the sixteenth century. Sultan Suleiman of Istanbul ruled millions of faithful Muslims. The Ottoman Empire conquered Arab lands, including what is now Iraq. The empire ended formally in 1918.

ratify To formally approve.

sanctions In the case of Iraq, restrictions on imports into the country during the 1990s, designed to limit Iraq's ability to develop weapons of mass destruction.

Scuds Missiles developed by the Soviet Union and modified by Iraq.

Shiite The majority Muslim sect in Iraq but a minority (less than 15 percent) worldwide.

Sunni The major division of Islam worldwide but a minority in Iraq.

UNSCOM The United Nations Special Commission on Iraq, created at the end of the first Gulf War for the purposes of identifying and destroying Iraq's chemical, biological, and missile capabilities.

WMD Weapons of mass destruction, including nuclear, chemical, and biological weapons capable of causing massive damage.

[FOR MORE] INFORMATION

Arms Control Association
1726 M Street NW
Washington, DC 20036
(202) 463-8270
Web site: http://www.armscontrol.org

Carnegie Endowment for International Peace
1779 Massachusetts Avenue NW
Washington, DC 20036
(202) 483-7600
Web site: http://www.ceip.org

Center for Defense Information
1779 Massachusetts Avenue NW
Washington, DC 20036
(202) 332-0600
Web site: http://www.cdi.org

Center for Nonproliferation Studies
460 Pierce Street
Monterey, CA 93940
(831) 647-4154
Web site: http://www.cns.miis.edu

Chemical and Biological Arms Control Institute
1747 Pennsylvania Avenue NW
Washington, DC 20006
(202) 296-3550
Web site: http://www.cbaci.org

Chemical and Biological Defense
Information Analysis Center
Aberdeen Proving Ground-Edgewood Area
P.O. Box 196
Gunpowder Branch APG, MD 21010-0196
(410) 676-9030
Web site: http://www.cbiac.apgea.army.mil

Federation of American Scientists
1717 K Street NW, Suite 209
Washington, DC 20036
(202) 546-3300
Web site: http://www.fas.org

Henry L. Stimson Center
11 Dupont Circle NW 9th Floor
Washington, DC 20036
(202) 223-5956
Web site: http://www.stimson.org

National Security Archive
Gelman Library, Suite 701
George Washington University
2130 H Street NW
Washington, DC 20037
(202) 994-7000
Web site: http://www.gwu.edu/~nsarchiv

Peace Action
1100 Wayne Avenue, Suite 1020
Silver Spring, MD 20910
(301) 565-4050
Web site: http://www.peace-action.org

Union of Concerned Scientists
2 Brattle Square
Cambridge, MA 02238
(617) 547-5552
Web site: http://www.ucsusa.org

United States Department of State
Bureau of Ams Control
2201 C Street NW
Washington, DC 20520
(202) 647-4000
Web site: http://www.state.gov/t/ac

WEB SITES

Due to to the changing nature of Internet links, the Rosen Publishing Group, Inc., has developed an online list of Web sites related to the subject of this book. This site is updated regularly. Please use this link to access the list:

http://www.rosenlinks.com/lwmd/swmdi

[FOR FURTHER]
READING

Bodnarchuk, Kari J. *Kurdistan: Region Under Siege*. Minneapolis: Lerner Publications Company, 2000.

Carlisle, Rodney P. *Persian Gulf War*. New York: Facts on File, 2003.

Foster, Leila M. *Iraq*. New York: Children's Press, 1998.

Hurley, Jennifer A., ed. *Weapons of Mass Destruction: Opposing Viewpoints*. San Diego: Greenhaven Press, 1999.

Levine, Herbert M. *Chemical & Biological Weapons in Our Times*. New York: Franklin Watts, 2000.

Nardo, Don. *The Persian Gulf War: The War Against Iraq*. San Diego: Lucent Books, 2001.

Norris, John and Will Fowler. *NBC: Nuclear, Biological & Chemical Warfare on the Modern Battlefield*. London: Brassey's, 1997.

Parks, Peggy. *Iraq*. Farmington Hills, MI: Blackbirch Press, 2003.

Pringle, Laurence. *Chemical and Biological Warfare: The Cruelest Weapons*, Revised edition. Berkeley Heights, NJ: Enslow Publishers, Inc. 2000.

Richie, Jason. *Iraq and the Fall of Saddam Hussein*. Minneapolis: The Oliver Press, Inc., 2003.

Rivera, Sheila. *Operation Iraqi Freedom*. Edina, MN: ABDO Publishing Company, 2004.

Roraback, Amanda. *Iraq in a Nutshell*. Santa Monica, CA: Enisen Publishing, 2003.

[BIBLIOGRAPHY]

Arnove, Anthony, ed. *Iraq Under Siege: The Deadly Impact of Sanctions and War*. Cambridge, MA: South End Press, 2000.

Clark, Wesley K. *Winning Modern Wars*. New York: Perseus Book Group, 2003.

Cockburn, Andrew and Patrick Cockburn. *Out of the Ashes: The Resurrection of Saddam Hussein*. New York: HarperCollins, 1999.

Cordesman, Anthony H. *The Iraq War: Strategy, Tactics, and Military Lessons*. Westport, CT: Praeger, 2003.

Hiro, Dilip. *Iraq: In the Eye of the Storm*. New York: Thunder Mouth Press/Nation Books, 2002.

Mackey, Sandra. *The Reckoning: Iraq and the Legacy of Saddam Hussein*. New York: W. W. Norton & Company, 2002.

Miller, Judith, Stephen Engelberg, and William Broad. *Germs: Biological Weapons and America's Secret War*. New York: Simon & Schuster, 2001.

Power, Samantha. *A Problem from Hell: America and the Age of Genocide*. HarperCollins, 2002.

Purdum, Todd S. and the staff of The New York Times. *A Time of Our Choosing: America's War in Iraq*. New York: Henry Holt and Company, 2003.

Silfry, Micah L., and Christopher Cerf, eds. *The Iraq War Reader: History, Documents, Opinion*. New York: Simon & Schuster, 2003.

Tragert, Joseph. *The Complete Idiot's Guide to Understanding Iraq*. Indianapolis, IN: Alpha Books, 2003.

Tripp, Charles. *A History of Iraq*. Cambridge, United Kingdom: Cambridge University Press, 2000.

[INDEX]

Kurds in, 10, 16, 18–19, 35, 39–43
missile program of, 30, 31–34, 43
nerve agents and, 38
UN inspections and, 23, 24, 31, 34,
    44, 52
UN sanctions and, 22, 23–24, 54
U.S. relations with, 4–6, 7, 13, 15,
    16–17, 19, 22, 23, 31, 36–37, 44,
    46, 53–54
Israel, 28, 29, 34

K
Kay, David, 52, 53
Khomeini, Ayatollah, 12–14
Kurds, 10, 16, 18–19, 35, 39–43
Kuwait, Iraq invasion of, 4–6, 17, 19, 23

M
Majid, "Chemical" Ali Hassan al-,
    41–43
missiles, 30, 31–34, 43, 44
Muslims
    Shia/Shiites, 10, 12, 14, 16, 43
    Sunnis, 10, 12, 14
Muthanna State Establishment, 38

N
nerve agents, 36, 37–38, 39
North Korea, 28
Nuclear Non-Proliferation Treaty, 28

O
oil, 8, 10–11, 13, 15, 19, 24, 36

R
Reagan, Ronald, 36–37

S
September 11, 2001, 24–26, 48

T
Tammuz I, 29, 31
terrorists, 7, 25–26, 48

U
United Nations (UN), 5, 6, 20,
    22, 32, 44, 54
United States
    Iran and, 13, 17, 23, 37
    Iraq and, 4--6, 13, 15, 16–17, 20,
        22, 23, 24, 31, 36–37, 44, 46,
        53–54
    weapons and, 27–28, 31, 32, 36
UN Resolution 687, 19, 20, 23,
    32–33, 44, 51
UN Special Commission
    (UNSCOM), 44, 51–52

W
Wolfowitz, Paul, 20, 23
World War I, 10, 36
World War II, 28, 36

ABOUT THE AUTHOR

This is Barbara Moe's nineteenth book for the Rosen Publishing Group. She is also the author of two young-adult novels and a chapter book. As a social worker, she is active in the democratic process and spent two years in the Peace Corps in Iran.

PHOTO CREDITS

Cover, p. 51 © AFP/Getty Images; pp. 4–5, 35 © Reuters/Corbis; pp. 7, 20–21 © Peter Turnley/Corbis; p. 9 Perry-Castañeda Library Map Collection; p. 10 ©Antonio Scorza/AFP/Getty Images; pp. 11, 12–13, 18, 27, 43, 47, 48–49 © AP/Wide World Photos; pp. 14–15 © Henri Bureau/Corbis Sygma; pp. 16–17 © Jacques Langevin/Corbis Sygma; p. 19 © Abbas/Magnum Photos; p. 22 © Ramzi Haidar/AFP/Getty Images; p. 25 © Jeff Christensen/Reuters/Corbis; p. 29 © UPI/Landov; p. 30 © KRT/Newscom; p. 32 © UN/Corbis/Sygma; p. 33 © Chris Bouroncle/AFP/Getty Images; p. 37 © UNSCOM/AP/Wide World Photos; p. 38 © Corbis Sygma; pp. 40–41 © UNSCOM/Getty Images; p. 41 (inset) © Karem Sahib/AFP/Getty Images; p. 42 © Ministry of Defense—Pool/AP/Wide World Photos; p. 45 © CIA/AP/Wide World Photos; p. 53 © Roll Call Photos/Newscom.

Designer: Evelyn Horovicz; Editor: Leigh Ann Cobb;
Photo Researcher: Amy Feinberg